博古通今学汉语丛书
Gems of the Chinese Language Through the Ages

歇后语 100
100 Chinese Two-Part Allegorical Sayings

尹斌庸　编著

佳　岑　翻译

欧阳毅　绘图

华语教学出版社

SINOLINGUA

First Edition   1999
Fifth printing   2006

ISBN 7－80052－710－7
Copyright 1999 by Sinolingua
Published by Sinolingua
24 Baiwanzhuang Road, Beijing 100037, China
Tel: (86) 10-68995871
Fax: (86) 10-68326333
Site : www.sinolingua.com.cn
E-mail:hyjx@ sinolingua.com.cn
Printed by Beijing Foreign Languages Printing House
Distributed by China International
Book Trading Corporation
35 Chegongzhuang Xilu, P.O. Box 399
Beijing 100044, China

Printed in the People's Republic of China

前　言

　　学习汉语的外国学生，当他们初步掌握了汉语的语音、词汇、语法和文字时，很想进一步提高自己的汉语水平。怎样提高呢？一件重要的事就是需要掌握一些汉语语言中最有特色的东西——例如典故、成语、谚语、歇后语。这些东西既和汉语汉字有密切关系，又和汉族的文化背景有密切关系。掌握了它们，不但能够丰富外国人汉语的表达能力，而且也能够增强他们汉语表达的民族特色。简而言之，他们所掌握的汉语就更像汉语了。这就为成为一个"中国通"迈出了重要的一步。

　　为以上目的，我们给这样的外国学生编了一套"博古通今学汉语丛书"，包括"典故 100"、"成语 100"、"谚语 100"和"歇后语 100"。

　　本套书精选汉语中最有价值的、常用的、表现力强的成语、谚语、歇后语、典故各 100 则。每则均附英文释义，每则配一幅精美插图，另有一些难解词语中英文注释。

Preface

What is the next step for a foreign student of the Chinese language after mastering the phonetics, grammar, and a fair amount of vocabulary? It is highly desirable to grasp something typical Chinese—like idioms, set phrases, proverbs or even the two-part allegorical sayings peculiar to Chinese. These idioms are so closely related to Chinese culture that once one has mastered them, one will not only be able to speak idiomatic Chinese and sound more like a native speaker, but also penetrate deeper into Chinese culture, and gradually become a "China Hand".

For this purpose, we have composed this *Gems of the Chinese Language Through the Ages* series, which comprises the following four books:

The Stories Behind 100 Chinese Idioms
100 Pearls of Chinese Wisdom
100 Common Chinese Idioms and Set Phrases
100 Chinese Two-Part Allegorical Sayings

These idioms and proverbs have been chosen for their frequency of use, practical value and expressiveness.

Each one is accompanied by an English translation and an appropriate illustration. Some obscure expressions are classified with the help of annotations in both Chinese and English.

目　录
Contents

前言 ···································· *1*

Preface ····························· 2

1. 矮子爬楼梯——步步登高 ················· 1

   A dwarf climbing a ladder—becoming higher with
   each step

2. 八仙过海——各显神通 ················· 3

   The Eight Immortals cross the sea—each displaying
   his or her special prowess

3. 半天空里挂口袋——装疯(风) ············· 5

   Hanging a bag in mid-air—holding the wind (feigning
   madness)

4. 半夜里偷桃吃——找软的捏 ··············· 7

   Stealing peaches at midnight—picking only the soft
   ones

5. 扁担没扎——两头失塌 ················· 9

   A shoulder pole carelessly loaded—both loads will
   fall off

6. 搽粉进棺材——死要面子 ················· 11

   Putting make-up on before entering the coffin—saving
   face even when dying

7. 茶壶里煮饺子——倒不出来 ················ 13
Boiling dumplings in a teapot—no way to get them out

8. 城门里扛竹竿——直进直出 ················ 15
Carrying a pole through a city gate—in and out in a straight line

9. 窗户上的纸——一戳就破 ················ 17
Paper window panes—torn by a touch

10. 打破沙锅——问(璺)到底 ················ 19
Breaking an earthenware pot—cracking down to the bottom (getting to the root of the matter)

11. 大姑娘坐花轿——头一回 ················ 21
A girl sitting in a bridal sedan chair—the very first time

12. 大热天穿棉袄——不是时候 ················ 23
Wearing a padded coat on a hot day—out of season

13. 大水冲倒龙王庙——一家人不认一家人 ········ 25
The Temple of the Dragon King washed away by a flood—not recognizing one's kinsman

14. 刀尖上翻筋斗——玩命 ················ 27
Turning somersaults on knives—playing with one's life

15. 电线杆当筷子——大材小用 ················ 29
Using telephone poles as chopsticks—putting much material to petty use

16. 擀面杖吹火——一窍不通 ················ 31
Using a rolling pin to blow a fire—totally impenetrable (a complete ignoramus)

17. 高射炮打蚊子——小题大做 ················· 33
Killing a mosquito with a cannon—making a mountain out of a molehill

18. 隔年的皇历——过时了 ················· 35
Last year's almanac—out of date

19. 狗拿耗子——多管闲事 ················· 37
A dog catching a mouse—poking one's nose into other people's business

20. 狗撵鸭子——呱呱叫 ················· 39
A duck chased by a dog—quacking at the top of its voice

21. 狗咬刺猬——无处下口 ················· 41
A dog snapping at a hedgehog—having nowhere to bite

22. 狗咬吕洞宾——不识好人心 ················· 43
A dog biting Lü Dongbin—not being able to recognize a kind-hearted man

23. 狗坐轿子——不识抬举 ················· 45
A dog sitting in a sedan chair—unable to appreciate a favor

24. 棺材里伸手——死要钱 ················· 47
A hand stretched from a coffin—asking for money even when dead

25. 韩信将兵——多多益善 ················· 49
Han Xin commanding troops—the more the better

26. 和尚打伞——无法（发）无天 ················· 51
A monk holding an umbrella—having neither hair

(law) nor sky (Providence)

27. 和尚的脑壳——没法(发) ················· 53
   A monk's head—with no hair (no way out)

28. 黄连树下弹琴——苦中作乐 ············· 55
   Playing the zither under a Chinese pistache tree—
   seeking happiness from bitterness

29. 黄鼠狼单咬病鸭子——该倒霉 ········· 57
   A sick duck bitten by a weasel—more bad luck

30. 黄鼠狼给鸡拜年——没安好心 ········· 59
   The weasel pays a New Year call on the hen—not
   with good intentions

31. 火烧眉毛——顾眼前 ····················· 61
   Eyebrows on fire—concentrate on immediate matters

32. 鸡蛋里挑骨头——故意找错 ············· 63
   Picking bones from eggs—finding fault deliberately

33. 姜太公钓鱼——愿者上钩 ··············· 65
   A fish jumping to Jiang Taigong's hookless and
   baitless line—a willing victim

34. 脚底上擦油——溜了 ····················· 67
   Putting grease onto one's soles—to slip away

35. 井里的蛤蟆——没见过大天 ············· 69
   A frog in a well—never having seen the whole sky

36. 孔夫子搬家——净是输(书) ·············· 71
   Confucius moves house—nothing but books (always
   lose)

37. 快刀打豆腐——两面光 ·················· 73
   Bean curd cut with a sharp knife—smooth on both

sides

38. 癞蛤蟆打哈欠——好大口气 ·················· 75
A toad yawns—a gaping mouth (talking big)

39. 癞蛤蟆想吃天鹅肉——痴心妄想 ·················· 77
A toad craving for swan's flesh—an impractical dream

40. 老虎戴佛珠——假装善人 ·················· 79
A tiger wearing a monk's beads—a vicious person pretending to be benevolent

41. 老虎的屁股——摸不得 ·················· 81
The buttocks of a tiger—cannot be touched

42. 老虎嘴上拔胡子——找死 ·················· 83
Pulling a tiger's whiskers—only to court death

43. 老鼠掉进书箱里——咬文嚼字 ·················· 85
A mouse in a bookcase—chewing up the pages

44. 老鼠过街——人人喊打 ·················· 87
A rat runs across the street—everyone joins the hue and cry

45. 老鼠爬秤钩——自己称自己 ·················· 89
A mouse climbs onto a steelyard hook—weighing itself in the balance (chanting the praises of oneself)

46. 老鼠钻进风箱里——两头受气 ·················· 91
A mouse in a bellows—pressed from both ends (blamed by both sides)

47. 老鼠钻牛角——此路不通 ·················· 93
A mouse in an ox horn—meeting a dead end

48. 老王卖瓜——自卖自夸 ·················· 95

Lao Wang selling melons—praising his own wares

49. 雷公劈豆腐——专找软的欺 ·················· 97
The God of Thunder cleaves a bean curd—seeking
out the soft and weak to bully

50. 聋子的耳朵——摆设 ·················· 99
A deaf man's ears—just for show

51. 搂草打兔子——顺手 ·················· 101
Raking the hay and catching the rabbit—with no
extra trouble

52. 马尾穿豆腐——提不起来 ·················· 103
Threading bean curd with a hair from a horse's tail
—impossible to lift it up

53. 猫哭老鼠——假慈悲 ·················· 105
A cat crying over a mouse's misfortune—sham mercy

54. 门缝里瞅人——把人看扁了 ·················· 107
Gazing at someone from behind a slightly opened door
—taking a narrow view of a person

55. 木匠戴枷——自作自受 ·················· 109
A carpenter in a cangue—suffering from one's own
endeavors

56. 泥菩萨过河——自身难保 ·················· 111
A clay Buddha crossing a stream—hardly able to
save itself

57. 螃蟹夹豌豆——连爬带滚 ·················· 113
A crab carrying a pea—crawling and rolling

58. 旗杆上挂灯笼——高明 ·················· 115
A lantern hung from a flagpole—high and bright

59. 骑驴看唱本——走着瞧 ·················· 117
Reading a book on donkey back—reading while
riding (wait and see)

60. 骑在老虎背上——身不由己 ·················· 119
Riding a tiger—having no control over oneself

61. 千里送鹅毛——礼轻情意重 ·················· 121
Travel a thousand miles to bestow a goose feather—
a small gift may be a token of profound friendship

62. 青石板上钉钉——不动 ·················· 123
Driving a nail into a stone slab—impossible to
penetrate

63. 秋后的蚂蚱——蹦跶不了几天 ·················· 125
A grasshopper at the end of autumn—its jumping
days are numbered

64. 热锅上的蚂蚁——团团转 ·················· 127
A swarm of ants on a hot oven—milling around in a
panic

65. 肉包子打狗——有去无回 ·················· 129
A meat bun thrown at a dog—by no means retrievable

66. 十五只吊桶打水——七上八下 ·················· 131
Fifteen buckets to draw water from a well—seven up
and eight down (all at sixes and sevens)

67. 寿星老上吊——嫌命长 ·················· 133
A person of longevity hangs himself—growing tired of
living a long life

68. 睡在磨盘上——想转了 ·················· 135
Sleeping on a millstone—expecting a turn of fortune

11

69. 孙猴子的脸——说变就变················ 137
The Monkey King's face—unpredictable changes

70. 太平洋上的警察——管得宽 ·············· 139
In charge of the Pacific Ocean—excessive
responsibilities

71. 太岁头上动土——好大的胆 ············· 141
Digging clay near Taisui—being reckless

72. 铁打的公鸡——一毛不拔 ·············· 143
An iron rooster—not a feather can be pulled out

73. 听评书掉眼泪——替古人担忧 ·········· 145
Shedding tears while listening to *pingshu*—worrying
about the ancients

74. 秃子跟着月亮走——沾光 ·············· 147
A bald head shines in the moonlight—reflected glory

75. 秃子头上的虱子——明摆着 ············ 149
A louse on a bald head—too obvious

76. 兔子的尾巴——长不了 ················ 151
A hare's tail—cannot be too long

77. 脱了裤子放屁——多费一道手续 ········ 153
Taking off the pants to break wind—make an
unnecessary move

78. 外甥打灯笼——照旧(舅) ·············· 155
The nephew holds a lantern for his uncle—things
stay unchanged

79. 王八吃秤砣——铁了心 ················ 157
A tortoise swallowing a weight—get an iron heart

80. 蚊子叮菩萨——认错人了 ·············· 159

A mosquito bites a clay idol—mistaken identity

81. 乌龟吃萤火虫——心里明白 ················ 161
A tortoise which has swallowed a firefly—bright inside

82. 瞎子戴眼镜——多此一举 ················ 163
A blind man putting on glasses—an unnecessary action

83. 瞎子点灯——白费蜡 ················ 165
A blind man lighting a candle—wasting wax

84. 虾子过河——谦虚(牵须) ················ 167
A shrimp crossing a river—modesty

85. 瞎子磨刀——快了 ················ 169
A blind man sharpening a knife—not far to go (it
feels sharper now)

86. 小葱拌豆腐——一清(青)二白 ················ 171
Shallot mixed with bean curd—one green and one
white (completely clear-cut or innocent)

87. 小孩儿放鞭炮——又爱又怕 ················ 173
Kids letting off firecrackers—feeling both joy and fear

88. 小和尚念经——有口无心 ················ 175
An apprentice monk reciting scriptures—saying what
one does not mean

89. 秀才遇见兵——有理说不清 ················ 177
A scholar meeting a warrior—unable to vindicate
oneself against an unreasonable opponent

90. 哑巴吃黄连——有苦说不出 ················ 179
A dumb person tasting bitter herbs—unable to
express bitter feelings

91. 哑巴吃饺子——心里有数 ················ 181

A mute person eating *jiaozi*—knowing how many
he has eaten

92. 阎王爷出告示——鬼话连篇 …………… 183
The King of Hell's announcement—a whole series
of lies

93. 张飞穿针——粗中有细 …………… 185
Zhang Fei threading a needle—subtle in one's rough
ways

94. 丈二金刚——摸不着头脑 …………… 187
The giant monk's head—cannot be reached (can't
make head or tail of something)

95. 芝麻开花——节节高 …………… 189
Sesame in bloom—rising steadily

96. 周瑜打黄盖——一个愿打,一个愿挨 …… 191
Zhou Yu beats Huang Gai—the punishment is
appropriately given by one and willingly accepted
by the other

97. 猪八戒吃人参果——全不知滋味 ………… 193
Zhu Bajie eating ginseng—not knowing the taste at all

98. 猪八戒照镜子——里外不是人 ………… 195
Zhu Bajie looking at himself in a mirror—blamed
everywhere

99. 竹篮打水——一场空 …………… 197
Drawing water with a bamboo basket—achieving nothing

100. 啄木鸟找食——全凭嘴 …………… 199
A woodpecker searching for food—all depending on
the mouth

矮子爬楼梯——步步登高

ǎizi pá lóutī——bùbù dēng gāo

A dwarf climbing a ladder — becoming higher with each step

个子矮的人想高一些,有一个很好的办法,就是爬梯子,爬一步高一步,这就是"步步登高"。

这个歇后语用来比喻人的官职、地位等由低到高步步提升;也比喻人的生活越来越好或成绩不断提高等。(含褒义)

A good way for a dwarf to get taller is to climb a ladder. Each step will make him look more exalted.

This expression means rising in rank or position step by step. It can also refer to the improvement of one's life or accumulation of achievements.

八仙过海——各显神通

bā xiān guò hǎi——gè xiǎn shéntōng

The Eight Immortals cross the sea—each displaying his or her special prowess

　　"八仙"是道教传说中的八个神仙：汉钟离、张果老、韩湘子、铁拐李、吕洞宾、曹国舅、蓝采和、何仙姑。有一次，八仙一同渡过大海。渡海时，他们各自显示出一套神奇的本事。

　　这个歇后语用来比喻在做某事时，各人有各人的一套办法；或者各人施展各人的才能，互相比赛。

The Eight Immortals of Taoism in Chinese folklore: Han Zhongli, Zhang Guolao, Han Xiangzi, Tieguai Li, Lü Dongbin, Cao Guojiu, Lan Caihe and He Xiangu. Once when they were crossing the sea together, they soared over it, each using his or her magic power.

This allegory is used to describe individuals who vie with each other by showing their special abilities, or each of them has a unique way to accomplish a task.

半天空里挂口袋——装疯（风）

bàntiānkōng li guà kǒudài——zhuāng fēng

Hanging a bag in mid-air — holding the wind (feigning madness)

这是一个谐音的歇后语。在半空中挂上一个大口袋，能用来干什么呢？只能用来装风。"疯"与"风"同音，"装风"就变成"装疯"。

"装疯"指一个人故意装作疯癫痴呆的样子。(含贬义)

When a bag is hung in mid-air, what can it hold? Only the wind. In Chinese, to hold the wind 装风 and to feign madness 装疯 sound the same.

This refers to someone who pretends to be insane.

半夜里偷桃吃——找软的捏

bànyè lǐ tōu táo chī——zhǎo ruǎn de niē

Stealing peaches at midnight—picking only the soft ones

生桃子不好吃,又酸又硬。成熟了的桃子一般都是软的,很甜很好吃。假如有一个人,半夜里去偷桃子,看不清哪个熟了哪个没熟,只好先捏一捏,软的桃子就成熟了。

这个歇后语用来比喻专门欺负弱小者,也就是"欺软怕硬"。(含贬义)

The raw peaches, hard and sour, are unpleasant to the taste, while ripe ones are normally soft and sweet. Imagine a person stealing peaches at midnight in darkness. He can only go by feel to find the soft ones.

This is a way of describing those who bully the weak and cringe before bullies.

扁担没扎——两头失塌

biǎndan méi zā——liǎng tóu shī tā

A shoulder pole carelessly loaded — both loads will fall off

扁担是用来挑东西的一种简单的工具。扁担的两端如果不扎住,挑起重担,两头的东西就会滑下去,叫做"两头失塌"。

这个歇后语用来比喻本想得到两个收获,结果却是两头落空。(含贬义)

When the loads at the ends of a shoulder pole are not attached properly, they will fall off.

This expression is used to allude negatively to those who want to kill two birds with one stone, only to lose both birds eventually.

搽粉进棺材——死要面子

chá fěn jìn guāncái——sǐ yào miànzi

Putting make-up on before entering the coffin— saving face even when dying

人快要死了，还要往脸上涂脂抹粉，再睡到棺材里去。

这个歇后语用来比喻条件不够时，还要极力维护自己的体面；或者极力装扮自己，掩盖丑恶的面目。(含贬义)

Some people, even on their death beds, still adorn themselves in order to look their best to the last.

This saying is used to satirize someone who is in disgrace or has something to be ashamed of but tries desperately to save face, or someone who tries hard to cover his ugliness or scandal by decking himself out.

茶壶里煮饺子——倒不出来

cháhú lǐ zhǔ jiǎozi——dào bù chūlái

Boiling dumplings in a teapot — no way to get them out

　　茶壶肚子大,口小。饺子放到茶壶里去煮,煮熟了,但因为口太小,饺子倒不出来。

　　这个歇后语用来比喻有的人肚子里有很多学问,或者是很想讲话,但是又不善于讲话,不能够把他的学识或想讲的话很好地表达出来。

A teapot has a big belly but a narrow spout. When dumplings are boiled in it, one can not pour them out through the spout like tea.

This idiom is used to describe a poor speaker who, despite all his learning and ideas, can't express himself eloquently.

城门里扛竹竿——直进直出

chéngmén li káng zhúgān——zhí jìn zhí chū

Carrying a pole through a city gate—in and out in a straight line

竹竿很长,城门很窄。在城门里扛竹竿,只能直着进去,直着出来,不能拐弯。

这个歇后语主要用来比喻说话办事不拐弯抹角,直截了当。(含褒义)有时也比喻说话办事粗心、简单。(含贬义)

As a pole is comparatively long and a city gate is narrow, one can only carry the pole straight in order to get through the gate.

This is a commendatory saying when referring to someone who is outspoken and comes straight to the point. However, it is derogatory when used to describe someone who is simply hasty and careless in speech or in action.

窗户上的纸——一戳就破

chuānghu shàng de zhǐ——yī chuō jiù pò

Paper window panes—torn by a touch

在玻璃还没有制造出来以前，人们普遍使用很薄的纸来糊窗户。薄薄的窗户纸，只要用手指头轻轻一戳就破了。

这个歇后语用来比喻稍加指点就明白了。

Before glass was invented, people in China used thin paper as window panes. Even a light touch could make a hole in the paper.

This expression indicates something which can be understood with a mere indication.

打破沙锅——问（璺）到底

dǎpò shāguō——wèn dào dǐ

Breaking an earthenware pot—cracking down to the bottom (getting to the root of the matter)

　　这是一个谐音歇后语。"璺"（wèn）是陶瓷、玻璃等器具上的裂痕。沙锅一打破，就从上面裂到底下，即"璺到底"。"问"和"璺"同音，"璺到底"变成"问到底"。

　　这个歇后语用来比喻追问一件事情，寻根刨（páo）底，非要弄清楚不可。

A crack in glassware or earthenware in Chinese, 璺, is pronounced the same as 问, to ask. So a crack in a broken earthenware pot which extends to the bottom 璺到底 sounds like 问到底, to question closely or to get to the root of the matter.

This metaphor is often used to describe one's determination to inquire deeply into something so as to get the final answer to a problem.

大姑娘坐花轿——头一回

dàgūniang zuò huājiào——tóu yī huí

A girl sitting in a bridal sedan chair—the very first time

按照过去的风俗,姑娘出嫁时都要坐花轿。坐花轿这件事对每一个姑娘来说,都是第一回。

这个歇后语用来比喻第一次做某一件事情,缺乏经验。

Traditionally, a bride was carried in a special sedan chair to the groom's home. So this was a first-time experience for every girl.

This allegory is used to refer to the first time one does something, implying a complete lack of experience.

大热天穿棉袄——不是时候

dà rètiān chuān mián´ǎo——bù shì shíhou

Wearing a padded coat on a hot day — out of season

冬天是穿棉袄的季节。如果有一个人,在大热天里穿着棉袄,这个人实在是太不合时宜了。

这个歇后语用来比喻说话、做事选择的时间不合适。(含贬义)

If a padded coat is worn in summer instead of winter, it is most inappropriate.

This expression is used to satirize untimeliness in speech or in action.

大水冲倒龙王庙——一家人不认一家人

dàshuǐ chōngdǎo lóngwángmiào——yī jiā rén bù rèn yī jiā rén

The Temple of the Dragon King washed away by a flood—not recognizing one's kinsman

　　龙王是传说中住在水域里的最高的神。龙王庙是供奉龙王的庙宇。发大水是归龙王管的。大水冲倒龙王庙是自家人不认识自家人的可笑结果。

　　这个歇后语用来比喻自己方面的人，由于互相不了解而发生误会或冲突。

In Chinese mythology, the god who controlled water was the Dragon King. So it would be ironic if a temple dedicated to the Dragon King should be destroyed by a flood.

This idiom is often cited when people of the same party or side misunderstand or conflict with each other.

刀尖上翻筋斗——玩命

dāojiān shàng fān jīndǒu——wánrmìng

Turning somersaults on knives — playing with one's life

翻筋斗应该在地上翻,假如有人为了逞能,要在刀尖上去翻筋斗。这不是拿生命开玩笑吗?这就叫"玩命"。

这个歇后语用来比喻去干非常冒险的事,随时可能丧失生命。(含贬义)

Normally one turns somersaults on the ground. So when someone tries to show off by turning somersaults on knives, he is simply gambling with his life.

This expression describes someone who risks his life needlessly.

电线杆当筷子——大材小用

diànxiàngān dàng kuàizi——dà cái xiǎo yòng

Using telephone poles as chopsticks — putting much material to petty use

中国人吃饭习惯用筷子。筷子是两根细小的竹棍或木棍。如果把又粗又大的电线杆当筷子使用,那岂不是大材料派小用场了吗?

这个歇后语多用来比喻人事安排上不合理,把有突出才能的人安排去干一般的工作,以致才能不能得到充分发挥。(含贬义)

Chopsticks are thin pieces of wood or bamboo, easy to manipulate with the hands. If huge poles were to be used for chopsticks, it would be a sheer waste of material.

This idiom is mostly used to refer to an unreasonable arrangement of personnel, i. e. sending a talented person to do a minor job, so that his talent is wasted.

擀面杖吹火———一窍不通

gǎnmiànzhàng chuī huǒ———yī qiào bù tōng

Using a rolling pin to blow a fire—totally impenetrable (a complete ignoramus)

　　"擀面杖"是擀面用的木棍,实心的,中间没有通气孔。用擀面杖去吹火,当然不能把火吹旺。"窍"就是窟窿、孔洞。

　　"一窍不通"也是一个成语,一般指对某种事物或某种技术一点也不懂,完全外行。

A rolling pin is a solid wooden stick used to roll dough. Since it does not have a hole, it naturally cannot be used to blow a fire. 窍 means hole or cavity.

一窍不通 is an idiom, meaning totally ignorant of a thing or a trade.

高射炮打蚊子——小题大做

gāoshèpào dǎ wénzi——xiǎo tí dà zuò

Killing a mosquito with a cannon — making a mountain out of a molehill

高射炮是用来打飞机的。几只小小的蚊子,却用高射炮向它们射击,这真是小问题花大力气。

"小题大做"的意思是:把小事情当做大事情来做,太不值得了。(含贬义)

A cannon is used to hit something huge, certainly not something as small as a mosquito.

This idiom is used to mean making a fuss over a trifle or giving too much importance to something small.

隔年的皇历——过时了

gé nián de huángli——guòshí le

Last year's almanac—out of date

　　口语上把历书叫"皇历"。一年一本皇历,新的一年到来,隔了一年的皇历就过时不能用了。

　　这个歇后语用来比喻过时的事物,再没有用了。(含贬义)

　　皇历　is often used colloquially to mean an almanac or calendar. When a year has passed, its calendar becomes useless.

　　This idiom is used to describe something out of date and no longer having any practical value.

狗拿耗子——多管闲事

gǒu ná hàozi——duō guǎn xiánshì

**A dog catching a mouse—poking one's nose into
other people's business**

　　耗子就是老鼠。捉老鼠本来是猫的事情,狗去捉老鼠,显然是多管闲事(与自己无关的事)。

　　这个歇后语用来比喻做与自己无关的,多余的事情,或做不应该做的事情。(含贬义)

It is a cat's business to catch mice, not a dog's.

This idiom is used to describe interference in someone else's affairs.

狗撵鸭子——呱呱叫

gǒu niǎn yāzi——guāguā jiào

A duck chased by a dog—quacking at the top of its voice

"撵"是追赶的意思。狗追赶鸭子的时候,鸭子就会发出"呱呱呱"的叫喊声。

"呱呱叫"在口语中用来形容极好,非常好,有夸奖的意思。本事大,能力强,事情做得很完美等,都可以用"呱呱叫"来形容。

撵 means to chase after or to drive away. When a dog is running after a duck, the duck will quack loudly 呱呱呱.

呱呱叫 in colloquial Chinese is often used to describe something excellent or someone who is very skillful and can accomplish something perfectly.

狗咬刺猬——无处下口

gǒu yǎo cìwei——wú chù xià kǒu

A dog snapping at a hedgehog—having nowhere to bite

刺猬是一种全身长着硬刺的小动物。刺猬遇到敌人时，便立刻缩成一团，像一个带刺的球一样。狗想咬刺猬，可是无论怎样也找不到下口的地方。

这个歇后语用来比喻做某种事情无从着手。

When a hedgehog meets an enemy, it rolls into a ball and shows its spines. So it is impossible for the enemy to bite it without being hurt.

This allegory means not knowing where to start or being in no position to accomplish something.

狗咬吕洞宾——不识好人心

gǒu yǎo Lǚ Dòngbīn——bù shí hǎorén xīn

A dog biting Lü Dongbin — not being able to recognize a kind-hearted man

　　吕洞宾是民间传说中的"八仙"之一。他常常帮助和救济别人,得到人们的喜爱。狗不认识吕洞宾这位神仙,把他当做坏人去咬,所以说它"不识好人心"。

　　这个歇后语用来比喻把别人的一片好心当做恶意,好坏不分。(含贬义)

One of the Eight Immortals, Lü Dongbin, often helped people, especially when they were in dire straits, so he was very popular. For a dog to bit Lü Dongbin would be to make a serious mistake.

This idiom is used to describe mistaking kindness for ill-intent.

狗坐轿子——不识抬举

gǒu zuò jiàozi——bù shí táiju

A dog sitting in a sedan chair—unable to appreciate a favor

"轿子"是从前的一种交通工具,方形,用竹子或木头制成,两边各有一根杆子,由人抬着走或由骡马驮着走。狗坐轿子里并不能认识到有人在抬着它和举着它。

"不识抬举"的意思是:不领会或者不接受别人对自己的好意。(含贬义)

A sedan chair was used by important people. If a dog were to ride in a sedan chair, it would not appreciate the privilege.

不识抬举 is an idiom, meaning unable to appreciate someone's kindness or favor.

棺材里伸手——死要钱

guāncai lǐ shēn shǒu——sǐ yào qián

A hand stretched from a coffin — asking for money even when dead

　　向人伸手,就有要钱的意思。已经装进棺材的死人,还向人伸出一只手,这不是"死要钱"吗?

　　"死要钱"形容贪财入迷,死了也不忘发财。讽刺惟利是图的人。(含贬义)

When a beggar stretches out his hand, he is asking for money. If a dead person lying in a coffin stretches out his hand to people, this can be interpreted as an excessively desperate gesture.

死要钱 means being overly greedy for money.

韩信将兵——多多益善

Hán Xìn jiàng bīng——duō duō yì shàn

Han Xin commanding troops—the more the better

　　韩信是汉朝皇帝刘邦手下的一名大将。将(jiàng)兵是带兵的意思。韩信擅长带兵,他认为,打仗时兵带得越多越好,有利于作战。

　　"多多益善"的意思是越多越好。这个歇后语比喻做事人越多越好,或使用的东西越多越好。(含褒义)

　　Han Xin was a famous general under Liu Bang, the first emperor of the Han Dynasty (206 B. C. -220 A. D.). When other people were afraid that too many troops were hard to control, Han Xin held confidently that the more troops he could command, the more advantages he had in a battle.

　　多多益善,the more the better, refers favorably to both the number of people and items one can use to do a job.

和尚打伞──无法(发)无天

héshang dǎ sǎn──wú fǎ wú tiān

A monk holding an umbrella — having neither hair (law) nor sky (Providence)

这是一个谐音的歇后语。和尚没有头发,所以说"无发"。"法"与"发"同音,(不同声调)即变成"无法"。和尚打着伞,伞遮住了天(无天),"和尚打伞"就是又"无法"(发),又"无天"。

"无法无天"的意思是:不受法纪的约束,毫无顾忌(jì)地胡作非为。(含贬义)

This is a pun. Monks shave their heads (发, hair, is pronounced the same as 法, law). Thus 无发, without hair, sounds the same as 无法, without law. When a monk holds an umbrella, it shields him from the sky, 天, above him, which also signifies Heaven or Providence.

无法无天 means running wild and defying all laws human and divine.

和尚的脑壳——没法(发)

héshang de nǎoké——méi fǎ

A monk's head—with no hair (no way out)

　　这是一个谐音的歇后语。和尚不留头发,所以是"没发"。"法"与"发"同音(不同音调),"没发"变成"没法"。

　　"没法"的意思是没有办法,没有门路。

This is also a pun.　A　monk's　head is without hair,　发,　a　similar sound to 法 which also means method or way.　Thus 没发, with no hair,　becomes 没法, meaning no way out,　or being able to do nothing about a situation.

黄连树下弹琴——苦中作乐

huángliánshù xià tánqín——kǔ zhōng zuòlè

Playing the zither under a Chinese pistache tree—seeking happiness from bitterness

黄连是一种非常苦的中草药。弹琴又是一件非常快乐的事情。在黄连树下弹琴,苦中取乐,形成有趣的对比。注意汉语中的"苦"有味苦(bitter)和痛苦(pain)两个意义。

"苦中作乐"的意思是在困苦的环境中寻求快乐。

The rhizome of Chinese goldthread which grows on Chinese pistache trees is an extremely bitter medicine, while playing the zither is a very enjoyable experience. So playing the instrument under such a tree makes an interesting contrast between bitterness and happiness. Note that 苦, bitter, can also mean pain.

苦 中 作 乐 means seeking happiness and pleasure in an adverse and painful environment.

黄鼠狼单咬病鸭子——该倒霉

huángshǔláng dān yǎo bìng yāzi——gāi dǎoméi

A sick duck bitten by a weasel—more bad luck

鸭子病了，已经不幸，偏偏又给黄鼠狼咬了，真该它倒霉。

这条歇后语用来比喻灾难偏偏落到不幸者的头上。

When a duck unfortunately gets sick, and then is caught by a weasel, the duck is really down on its luck.

This idiom describes someone who has already suffered a misfortune and then meets another disaster.

黄鼠狼给鸡拜年——没安好心

huángshǔláng gěi jī bàinián——méi ān hǎoxīn

The weasel pays a New Year call on the hen—not with good intentions

黄鼠狼又叫黄鼬（yòu），白天睡觉，晚上出来活动，常常危害鸡鸭等家禽。黄鼠狼明明想把鸡吃掉，却装模作样给鸡拜年，这显然是不怀好意（没安好心）。

这个歇后语比喻表面上亲热和善，实际上居心险恶。

The weasel usually sleeps during the day and goes out at night, praying on chickens, ducks and the like. So if a weasel pays a hen a New Year call, obviously it has a hidden motive.

This idiom is used to describe a hypocrite, who seems kind and sincere but is actually malignant and vicious.

火烧眉毛——顾眼前

huǒ shāo méimao——gù yǎnqián

Eyebrows on fire — concentrate on immediate matters

眉毛在眼睛的上边，紧挨着眼睛。眉毛失了火，眼睛就很危险了。

这个歇后语用来比喻情况非常急迫，必须先解决当前的问题，其他事暂时放在一边。也比喻眼光短浅，只顾眼前，不顾将来。

Since the eyebrows are immediately above the eyes, when the eyebrows are on fire, the eyes are in immediate danger. 眼前, before or above the eyes, also means right now, at present.

This idiom is used when the circumstances have become desperately urgent and one must solve the most pressing problem, leaving aside other, less-important business. Sometimes it can also refer to shortsightedness, i. e. paying attention only to the present, without any consideration for the future.

鸡蛋里挑骨头——故意找错

jīdàn lǐ tiāo gǔtou——gùyì zhǎo cuòr

Picking bones from eggs—finding fault deliberately

　　鸡蛋里面本来是没有骨头的，有人偏要在鸡蛋里挑出一块骨头来,这意味着什么呢?

　　这个歇后语用来比喻故意挑剔别人的缺点和错误,也就是无中生有,硬挑毛病。(含贬义)

Someone who tries to pick bones from an egg is trying to find something which is not there.

This allegory refers to someone who is hypercritical and likes to fabricate something out of nothing.

姜太公钓鱼——愿者上钩

Jiāngtàigōng diàoyú——yuàn zhě shàng gōu

A fish jumping to Jiang Taigong's hookless and baitless line—a willing victim

中国周朝初年,有个叫姜子牙的人,隐居在陕西的渭水河边几十年,常用无诱饵的直钩在水边钓鱼。姜子牙的目的不在钓鱼,而是希望有人请他出去,施展他的政治抱负。后来在他年纪很老的时候,终于实现了自己的理想。人们尊称他为"姜太公"。

"愿者上钩"用来比喻心甘情愿地去干某件事情(多指上当受骗一类事情)。

In the first years of the Zhou Dynasty, a hermit, Jiang Ziya, was often seen fishing in the River Wei in Shaanxi Province. What was peculiar about him was that his line was hookless and baitless, for he was simply waiting to be invited to take an official post. This ambition was finally realized in his old age, and he was respectfully addressed as Jiang Taigong (Taigong literally means great-grandfather).

This saying refers to someone who willingly plays into other people's hands and, more often than not, becomes a victim.

脚底上擦油——溜了

jiǎodǐ shàng cā yóu——liū le

Putting grease onto one's soles—to slip away

动词"溜"有两个意思：一个是滑行，另一个是偷偷地走开。脚底擦了油，走起路来很滑，所以说是"溜了"，这里是第一个意思。运用的时候采用第二个意思，比喻有的人遇到困难的事或对自己不利的事，就采取"溜"的办法。即偷偷地走开或不声不响地离开。（含贬义）

The character 溜 has two meanings: to slide and to sneak off. Grease on one's soles makes one liable to slip. But it is the second meaning that the pun is aimed at, i. e. when someone meets with difficulties or is caught in an unfavorable situation, he tends to slip away.

井里的蛤蟆——没见过大天

jǐng lǐ de háma——méi jiànguo dà tiān

A frog in a well—never having seen the whole sky

居住在井里的蛤蟆,没法跳出水井,只能看到井口那么大的一点天空,不知道天空到底有多大。

这个歇后语用来讽刺那些眼界狭小,见识有限的人。(含贬义)

A frog living in a well can only see the part of the sky framed by the mouth of the well.

This idiom is used to ridicule short-sighted and narrow-minded people.

孔夫子搬家——净是输（书）

Kǒng fūzǐ bānjiā——jìng shì shū

Confucius moves house — nothing but books (always lose)

这是一个谐音歇后语。孔夫子是中国儒家学说的创始人。人们认为他最有学问，家中的书当然很多了。孔夫子搬家，搬的都是书。"输"与"书"同音，""净是书"变成了"净是输"。

这个歇后语用来比喻总是失败。

Confucius, the founder of the Confucian school, was considered the most learned scholar in ancient China, so there must have been a great number of books in his home. When he moved house, what he took with him was probably mostly books. 书, book, however, sounds the same as 输, to lose.

This pun means always losing out.

快刀打豆腐——两面光

kuài dāo dǎ dòufu——liǎng miàn guāng

Bean curd cut with a sharp knife — smooth on both sides

用一把锋利的刀（快刀）劈开豆腐，劈开的两个面都是光光滑滑的。这就是"两面光"。

"两面光"是处世圆滑的一种表现。

When a sharp knife is used to cut bean curd, the two sides left after the cut will both look very smooth.

两面光 is a common saying, meaning trying to please both parties, or being slick and sly.

癞蛤蟆打哈欠——好大口气

làiháma dǎ hāqian——hǎo dà kǒuqì

A toad yawns—a gaping mouth (talking big)

癞蛤蟆就是蟾蜍（chánchú）。他本来就有一张大嘴巴，在打哈欠的时候，他的嘴巴更显得大了。

"好大口气"用来讽刺喜欢说大话，吹牛皮的人。（含贬义）

A toad has a huge mouth. When it yawns, its mouth becomes even bigger.

好大口气 is often cited to ridicule a boastful person.

癞蛤蟆想吃天鹅肉——痴心妄想

làiháma xiǎng chī tiān´é ròu——chīxīn wàngxiǎng

A toad craving for swan's flesh—an impractical dream

又美丽又高雅的天鹅在空中飞，又丑陋又笨拙的癞蛤蟆在地上爬。癞蛤蟆忽然想起要是能吃到天鹅的肉，那该多好啊。但这是实现不了的痴心和妄想。

这个歇后语用来讥笑某些人不切实际的过高愿望。（含贬义）

The swan, so beautiful and refined, flies high in the sky, while the toad, so ugly and awkward, can only crawl on the earth. It would be hopelessly impractical for a toad to yearn for a taste of swan's flesh.

This is a very common saying, used to mock wishful thinking or impractical plans.

老虎戴佛珠——假装善人

lǎohǔ dài fózhū——jiǎzhuāng shànrén

A tiger wearing a monk's beads—a vicious person pretending to be benevolent

　　"佛珠"是佛教徒戴在脖子上，念经时用以计算次数的成串珠子。一贯吃人的老虎居然戴上佛珠，装扮起善人的模样来了。这个歇后语用来比喻坏人伪装成好人，或假发慈悲。（含贬义）

How can a carnivore like a tiger become a vegetarian like a monk simply by wearing prayer beads round its neck?

　　This expression is used to allude to people who pretend to be philanthropists but who are actually just the opposite, or a person pretending to be kind and benevolent.

老虎的屁股——摸不得

lǎohǔ de pìgu——mō bù dé

The buttocks of a tiger—cannot be touched

老虎是一种猛兽,惹了他是要吃人的。摸老虎的屁股去激怒他,是不会有好下场的。这个歇后语常用来比喻某些人依仗权势,作威作福;或者某人很厉害,别人一点也触犯不得。(含贬义)

Touching the buttocks of a tiger is a very dangerous act.

This common saying is used to describe someone with power and position who rides roughshod over the people, or someone who is too tyrannical to allow any comment or criticism of his actions.

老虎嘴上拔胡子——找死

lǎohǔ zuǐ shàng bá húzi——zhǎo sǐ

Pulling a tiger's whiskers—only to court death.

到老虎嘴巴上去拔胡子，很有可能被老虎吃掉，是一件十分危险的事。

这个歇后语用来比喻冒极大的危险去触犯强者。（含贬义）

If one pulls a tiger's whiskers one may end up inside the animal's mouth.

This idiom means taking a great risk by offending an authority or someone much more powerful than oneself.

老鼠掉进书箱里——咬文嚼字

lǎoshǔ diàojìn shūxiāng lǐ——yǎo wén jiáo zì

A mouse in a bookcase—chewing up the pages

老鼠的牙齿总是不停地咬东西，老鼠掉进书箱里，咬的都是书本，所以说它"咬文嚼字"。"咬文嚼字"多用来讥笑死抠（kōu）字眼，而不领会精神实质的书呆子。有时也用来讥笑那些故意卖弄自己学问的人。（含贬义）

If a mouse gets into a bookcase, what else can it do besides nibbling at the books?

This phrase is mostly used sarcastically to ridicule a pedant who is over-fastidious about wording but fails to grasp the essence of a text. Sometimes it refers to someone who parades his vocabulary just to show off.

老鼠过街——人人喊打

lǎoshǔ guò jiē——rénrén hǎn dǎ

A rat runs across the street—everyone joins the hue and cry

　　人们一般都认为老鼠是一个很坏的东西。如果他从大街上走过，街上的人都会大声喊："打死它！"

　　这个歇后语用来比喻害人的东西，人人痛恨。(含贬义)

This metaphor describes an evildoer who is hated by everyone.

老鼠爬秤钩——自己称自己

lǎoshǔ pá chènggōu——zìjǐ chēng zìjǐ

A mouse climbs onto a steelyard hook—weighing itself in the balance (chanting the praises of oneself)

秤（chèng）是测定物体重量的器具。秤杆上的金属钩子,是用来挂所称（chēng）物体的。老鼠爬到秤钩上,是自己称（chēng）自己的重量。"称（chēng）"有"测定重量"的意思,另外还有"称赞"的意思。"自己称自己"就是自己称赞或夸耀自己。

这个歇后语用来比喻没有什么本事的人自我吹嘘。（含贬义）

秤, when pronounced in the fourth tone (chèng), is a balance or steelyard. When a mouse climbs onto a steelyard hook, it is weighing, or in Chinese, 称 (chēng), itself. 称 (chēng), however, can also mean to praise. So 自己称自己 means to chant the praises of oneself.

This saying refers to a person who has no real ability but likes to boast of his prowess.

老鼠钻进风箱里——两头受气

lǎoshǔ zuānjìn fēngxiāng lǐ——liǎngtóu shòuqì

**A mouse in a bellows—pressed from both ends
(blamed by both sides)**

风箱是一种压缩空气、产生气流的装置，一头进气，一头出气，用来使炉火旺盛。假如老鼠钻到风箱里，无论跑到哪一头，都处在气流中，所以说是"两头受气"。

"受气"有受到欺侮的意思。"两头受气"比喻受到两方面的抱怨或责难。

A bellows works by inducting air at one end and expelling it from the other. If a mouse gets into it, it cannot escape the pressure of the air, which in Chinese is literally 受气.

Here 受气 actually means to be bullied. 两头受气 means being blamed by both sides.

老鼠钻牛角———此路不通

lǎoshǔ zuān niújiǎo———cǐ lù bù tōng

A mouse in an ox horn—meeting a dead end

with no way out.

　　牛角下头粗，上头尖。假如老鼠钻到牛角里，越往里面空间越小，最后没有路可走。

　　这个歇后语用来比喻某种办法或某种想法在现实中行不通。也比喻陷入绝境，无路可走。

Since an ox horn tapers toward the end, a mouse crawling into it will find itself increasingly hampered, until it meets a dead end.

This idiom is used to mean that an idea or method is not feasible or someone is in a tight spot with no way out.

老王卖瓜——自卖自夸

Lǎo Wáng mài guā——zì mài zì kuā

Lao Wang selling melons — praising his own wares

老王是一个假定卖瓜的人。老王卖瓜，一边卖，一边夸自己的瓜甜，这是招揽(lǎn)生意，希望有更多的人来买他的瓜。

这个歇后语用来比喻自吹自擂，自己夸耀自己。(含贬义)

Lao Wang is the archetypal melon peddler, who naturally boasts how fine his melons are.

This idiom is often quoted to describe a person who likes to boast about his own exploits.

雷公劈豆腐──专找软的欺

léigōng pī dòufu──zhuān zhǎo ruǎn de qī

The God of Thunder cleaves a bean curd—seeking out the soft and weak to bully

　　豆腐很软,非常容易劈开。雷工是神话中传说专管打雷的神, 样子很凶恶。雷公用雷电去劈豆腐,比喻专找老实人或软弱的人欺负。(含贬义)

Bean curd is soft and very easy to cut, while the God of Thunder is the epitome of savage power.

This idiom implies choosing to bully only the vulnerable and weak.

聋子的耳朵——摆设

lóngzi de ěrduo——bǎishè

A deaf man's ears—just for show

聋子虽然也长着两只耳朵，可是听不到声音。所以这两只耳朵就好像一种摆设，不起任何作用。

"摆设"指那些只能装装样子，而毫无实用价值的东西。这个歇后语用来比喻虚有其表或徒有其名而实际不起作用的人或事物。(含贬义)

A deaf man cannot hear, despite having ears like other people. In this sense, his ears can be regarded as ornaments without any practical use.

摆设 means things merely for show and without pragmatic value.

This saying refers to someone or something that has a fine appearance but no substantial content or something that enjoys an undeserved reputation, despite its worthlessness.

搂草打兔子——顺手

lōu cǎo dǎ tùzi——shùn shǒu

Raking the hay and catching the rabbit—with no extra trouble

兔子藏在草丛里，搂草打兔子是顺手就能干的。指做一件事时，顺便又做了别的事。

Since rabbits usually hide themselves in thick grass or hay, when one is raking hay, he may easily catch a rabbit.

This expression means while doing something, one can conveniently accomplish something else without extra effort.

马尾穿豆腐——提不起来

mǎyǐ chuān dòufu——tí bù qǐlái

Threading bean curd with a hair from a horse's tail—impossible to lift it up

豆腐很软很嫩,轻轻一碰就会碎裂,用马尾巴上的毛来穿豆腐,是不可能把它提起来的。

"提不起来"常用来表示:(1)某人的能力、水平太低,无法提拔或培养;(2)精神或劲头不足,无法提起来。(含贬义)

Bean curd is so soft and delicate that it crumbles easily, even at a touch. Therefore, it is impossible to thread bean curd with a hair from a horse's tail.

提不起来 is often used to describe either someone who is too backward to be cultivated and improved or the state of lacking energy and spirit.

马尾(yǐ):特指马尾(wěi)巴上的毛。

马尾 refers to the hair on the tail of a horse.

猫哭老鼠——假慈悲

māo kū lǎoshǔ——jiǎ cíbēi

A cat crying over a mouse's misfortune—sham mercy

　　猫的本性是要吃老鼠的。假如有一只猫，居然同情和怜悯老鼠的遭遇而掉下眼泪，那一定是假装慈悲了。

　　这个歇后语用来比喻内心残忍而伪装仁慈善良的人。（含贬义）

A cat is a mouse's natural enemy. If a cat sheds tears at a mouse's misfortune, it must be only pretending to pity it. This saying is used to describe those who are ruthless inside but put on a show of benevolence.

门缝里瞅人——把人看扁了

ménfèng lǐ chǒu rén——bǎ rén kàn biǎn le

Gazing at someone from behind a slightly opened door—taking a narrow view of a person

瞅是看的意思。把门打开很小一条缝隙
(fèngxì),从缝隙中看人,人的形象就显得扁了。

"把人看扁了"是看不起人或小看别人的意
思。(含贬义)

瞅 means to look at, to gaze at. If one opens a
door slightly and gazes at someone through the
resultant crack, the attitude is the same as looking
down upon that person.

木匠戴枷──自作自受

mùjiang dài jiā──zì zuò zì shòu

A carpenter in a cangue—suffering from one's own endeavors

　　枷是过去套在罪犯脖子上的一种刑具，一般用木板制成。木匠自己制作了枷,后来却戴在自己的脖子上,这就是"自作自受"。

　　这个歇后语用来比喻自己做错事或坏事，自己去承受不好的后果。(含贬义)

A cangue was a kind of instrument of punishment consisting of a heavy wooden board hung round the neck. They were, of course, made by carpenters.

This saying is used to mean suffering the unfavorable consequences of one's own wrongdoing or mistake.

泥菩萨过河——自身难保

ní púsà guò hé——zìshēn nán bǎo

A clay Buddha crossing a stream—hardly able to save itself

在人们的心目中,菩萨是拯(zhěng)救危难的神。可是,用泥巴做成的菩萨,在过河的时候,一旦进入水里自身就会被河水溶化, 哪里还能去保佑别人呢?

这个歇后语用来比喻自己都难以保住,不能顾得上帮助别人。(含贬义)

Buddha is considered to be the supreme savior. However, a clay statue of Buddha will dissolve if it crosses a steam. How can it help others?

This saying denotes those who cannot even help themselves, not to mention others.

螃蟹夹豌豆——连爬带滚

pángxiè jiā wāndòu——lián pá dài gǔn

A crab carrying a pea—crawling and rolling

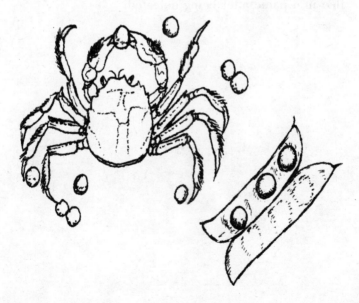

螃蟹走路时横着爬行。豌豆是又小又圆的东西。螃蟹要夹住豌豆实在不太容易,所以螃蟹夹豌豆的结果只能是一个爬,一个滚。

"连爬带滚"大多用来形容失败后惊慌逃跑的样子。

A crab scuttles sideways. It is extremely difficult for a crab to carry a pea, as one is crawling while the other is rolling.

This saying is often used to describe those who flee in a panic after being defeated.

旗杆上挂灯笼——高明

qígān shang guà dēnglong——gāomíng

A lantern hung from a flagpole—high and bright

　　把灯笼挂在很高很高的旗杆上点亮，灯笼又"高"又"明亮"。

　　"高"和"明"两个字合起来构成一个新的词"高明"，用来形容某个人的技能高于一般人。(含褒义)

A lighted lantern could be both 高 (high) and 明 (bright) when hung from a tall flagpole. 高明 is an expression that means wise, or skilled above average.

骑驴看唱本——走着瞧

qí lǘ kàn chàngběn——zǒuzhe qiáo

Reading a book on donkey back—reading while riding (wait and see)

"唱本"是刊载曲艺或戏曲唱词的小册子。骑在毛驴的背上看唱本,一边走,一边看。"一边走,一边看"是"走着瞧"的表面意思。

"走着瞧"的实际意思是:事情发展的结果如何(比如谁胜谁负),等着以后慢慢看。

唱本 is a brochure recording the words of Chinese ballad singing or traditional Chinese opera. Reading such a book while riding a donkey evokes an image of letting matters take their course.

走着瞧 in Chinese means the same as "wait and see". The actual meaning is that it takes some time to see the result of the development of some event.

骑在老虎背上——身不由己

qí zài lǎohǔ bèi shang——shēn bù yóu jǐ

Riding a tiger—having no control over oneself

一个人如果骑到了老虎的脊背上，要想下来可就困难了，只好由老虎带着跑，完全失去了自由。

这个歇后语用来比喻受别人控制，由不得自己做主。

When one rides a tiger one dare not dismount for fear of being eaten.

This saying is used to describe the situation of being deprived of freedom by exterior forces.

千里送鹅毛——礼轻情意重

qiān lǐ sòng émáo——lǐ qīng qíngyì zhòng

Travel a thousand miles to bestow a goose feather — a small gift may be a token of profound friendship

"千里"形容路途遥远。从遥远的地方送来一片鹅毛,东西虽然很轻,但是它代表的情意却很浓重。

这个歇后语用来比喻礼品虽然不多,但表达了送礼人的一片深情厚意。(含褒义)

Traveling a long way just to give somebody a goose feather indicates a profound friendship.

This saying is used to express that true friendship is not measured in terms of money or expensive gifts.

青石板上钉钉——不动

qīngshíbǎn shang dìng dīng——bù dòng

Driving a nail into a stone slab—impossible to penetrate

前一个"钉"（dìng）是动词，后一个"钉"（dīng）是名词。在坚硬的石板上钉钉子，钉子是钉不进去的，也就是"钉（dìng）不动"。

这个歇后语用来比喻事情发展已成定局，基本上不会再发生变动。

The first 钉 is a verb, while the second one is a noun. A nail cannot penetrate a stone slab, no matter how hard one drives it. In Chinese it is called 钉不动, which means that it is impossible to drive a nail into something.

The extended meaning of this idiom is that things are already settled and cannot be changed.

秋后的蚂蚱——蹦跶不了几天

qiū hòu de màzha——bèngda bù liǎo jǐ tiān

A grasshopper at the end of autumn—its jumping days are numbered

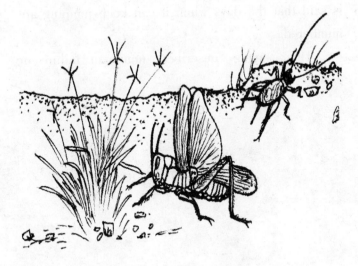

"蚂蚱"就是"蝗虫"。"蹦跶"就是"蹦跳"的意思。秋天过去,冬天马上就到了。蚂蚱到了秋后,活命的日子就不长了,所以说它"蹦跶不了几天"。

这个歇后语用来比喻离失败或灭亡没有多久了。(含贬义)

蚂蚱 means grasshopper. Similar to 蹦跳 in meaning, the English equivalent of 蹦达 is "jump". When winter takes the place of autumn, the grasshopper is also coming to the end of its life. So it is said that the days when it can keep jumping are numbered.

This saying describes imminent failure or destruction.

热锅上的蚂蚁——团团转

règuō shang de mǎyǐ——tuántuán zhuàn

A swarm of ants on a hot oven—milling around in a panic

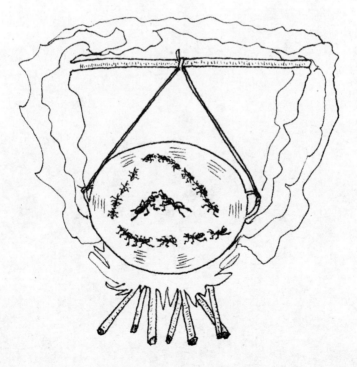

烧得灼 (zhuó) 热的铁锅上有一群蚂蚁，围着锅圈转来转去，想逃命，又没有办法逃走。

这个歇后语用来比喻陷入困境，走投无路。也用来描述心情焦急、坐立不安的状态。

A swarm of ants on a hot oven dash around, with no way out. This saying is used to describe people who are in a blind panic.

肉包子打狗——有去无回

ròu bāozi dǎ gǒu——yǒu qù wú huí

A meat bun thrown at a dog—by no means retrievable

　　狗很喜欢吃肉。用肉做的包子打狗,等于给狗送好吃的东西,扔出去当然就回不来了。

　　这个歇后语用来比喻东西放出去后收不回来。

There is no way of getting back a meat bun thrown at a dog in an attempt to drive it away.

Something given out but hardly returnable or someone going without coming back is often compared to a meat bun thrown at a dog.

十五只吊桶打水——七上八下

shíwǔ zhī diàotǒng dǎ shuǐ——qī shàng bā xià

Fifteen buckets to draw water from a well—seven up and eight down (all at sixes and sevens)

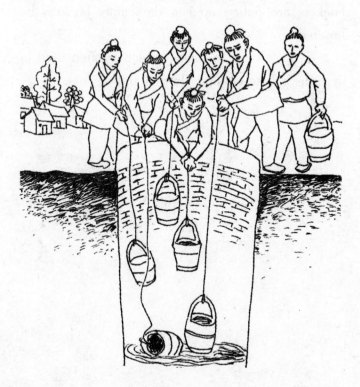

过去没有自来水,用水要到井里去提。在桶上绑根绳子吊下井去,水满后再提上来。设想用十五只吊桶轮番提水,七个桶吊上来,八个桶放下去。

"七上八下"也是个成语,常用来描述心神慌乱、不安。

In the past, when there was no tap-water, water had to be drawn from wells. Only when the full buckets are pulled up can the empty buckets be lowered.

七上八下 is an idiom, which is often used to describe a state of being flurried and restless.

寿星老上吊——嫌命长

shòuxinglǎo shàngdiào——xián mìng cháng

A person of longevity hangs himself — growing tired of living a long life

　　"寿星"就是"老人星",民间把他作为长寿的象征,也称为"寿星公"、"寿星老"。假如寿星老突然要上吊寻死,大家不禁会议论:"这老头子是不是嫌自己活得太长了?"

　　这歇后语用来比喻自己不知道保重自己的身体和性命,盲目去冒风险或硬打硬拼。(含贬义)

　　寿星, also called 寿星公 or 寿星老, refers to a person of longevity, and is regarded in Chinese culture as a symbol of long life.

　　If a person of longevity tried to hang himself or herself, it would indicate being tired of living.

　　This saying is used to refer to those who take risks blindly or fight recklessly without caring about their own health or lives.

睡在磨盘上——想转了

shuì zài mòpán shang——xiǎng zhuàn le

Sleeping on a millstone—expecting a turn of fortune

这个磨盘就是方言中说的磨，是一种把粮食弄碎的工具，磨盘转动，粮食才能压碎。人睡在磨盘上面，大概也想随着转动了。

"想转了"的意思是想偏了，想错了；另外也表示想开了，想明白了。

磨 is a millstone, used to grind grain into flour. Only when the millstone is turned can the grain be ground. If someone sleeps on a millstone, it indicates that he wants to turn with it.

想转了 implies thinking the wrong way. It may also mean looking on the bright side of things.

孙猴子的脸——说变就变

Sūn Hóuzi de liǎn——shuō biàn jiù biàn

The Monkey King's face—unpredictable changes

　　中国著名神话小说《西游记》中的孙悟空又称"孙猴子"，有七十二种变化的本领，只要一念咒语，说变什么就变什么。

　　这个歇后语用来比喻情况变化迅速，难以预料。

In *Journey to the West*, one of the four major classical Chinese novels, the main character Sun Wukong, also known as the Monkey King, has the power of 72 metamorphoses.

This saying is used to describe sudden unpredictable changes.

太平洋上的警察——管得宽

Tàipíng Yáng shang de jǐngchá——guǎn de kuān

In charge of the Pacific Ocean—excessive responsibilities

太平洋是世界上最大的海洋,广阔无边。假设在太平洋上当警察,管的地方就很宽很宽了。

"管得宽"指不该管或不需要管的事情也去管,操多余的心。(含贬义)

The Pacific is the largest ocean in the world. If a person were put in charge of the Pacific, he would have to govern a vast area too big to control properly.

管得宽 means the same as "have one's finger in every pie."

太岁头上动土——好大的胆

tàisuì tóu shang dòng tǔ——hǎo dà de dǎn

Digging clay near Taisui—being reckless

"太岁"是传说中的神名。过去迷信的说法认为太岁之神在地，掘土兴建工程要躲避太岁的方位,否则就要招来祸害。居然在太岁的头上动起土来,这不是自找灾祸吗?

"太岁头上动土"比喻去触犯有权势和强有力的人,胆子不小。(含贬义)

Taisui is the name of a god in Chinese mythology. As he lived below the ground, it was important not to dig for clay or engage in construction in his location. Otherwise, one risked disaster.

This idiom is used to refer to reckless actions, especially when one risks offending a person of power and influence.

铁打的公鸡——一毛不拔

tiě dǎ de gōngjī——yī máo bù bá

An iron rooster—not a feather can be pulled out

在公鸡身上拔毛本来是很容易的事情，然而要在铁铸成的公鸡身上拔下毛来，就不可能了。"一毛不拔"是一根毛也拔不下来的意思。

这个歇后语用来比喻一个人非常自私、吝啬，一点财物也不愿意拿出来。（含贬义）

It is an easy job to pluck a feather from a live rooster; but it is impossible to do so from one made of iron.

This saying refers to someone who is stingy and miserly, or a person who will not lift a finger to help.

听评书掉眼泪——替古人担忧

tīng píngshū diào yǎnlèi——tì gǔrén dānyōu

Shedding tears while listening to *pingshu*—worrying about the ancients

"评书"是曲艺的一种，讲的大多是古代的故事。听评书听到悲惨的地方，流下眼泪来，替故事里的人物(古人)着急、担忧。

这个歇后语用来比喻对毫不相干的人或事，产生不必要的忧虑。

Pingshu is a traditional Chinese story-telling art form. The themes are usually ancient ones. Shedding tears while listening to the sad part really shows great concern and worry about the ancients — the characters in the story.

This saying refers to unnecessary worries about persons or irrelevant things.

秃子跟着月亮走——沾光

tūzi gēnzhe yuèliang zǒu——zhānguāng

A bald head shines in the moonlight—reflected glory

"秃子"指头发掉光了的人。秃子在月亮下面走路,月亮的光照到秃子头上,秃子的头上也发亮了,是沾了月亮的光。

这个歇后语用来比喻凭借别人或某种事物而得到好处。(含贬义)

秃子 means a person with a bald head. In the moonlight, a bald man's head shines. The bald man borrows the natural light of the moon.

This saying implies gaining benefit from association with somebody or something.

秃子头上的虱子——明摆着

tūzi tóu shang de shīzi——míngbǎizhe

A louse on a bald head—too obvious

　　秃子的头上光光的,一根头发也没有。如果秃子头上有虱子,一眼就可以看到,因为它很明显地"摆"(放)在那里。

　　"明摆着"的意思是问题或事情很明显。

Since there is no hair on a bald head, a louse on it must be very conspicuous.

明摆着 means obvious, clear, plain.

兔子的尾巴——长不了

tùzi de wěiba——cháng bù liǎo

A hare's tail—cannot be too long

兔子的尾巴生来就很短,不可能再长(zhǎng)长(cháng)了。

这个歇后语用来比喻时间不会长久了（多指坏人、坏事）。（含贬义）

A hare is born with a short tail, which cannot grow long.

With the implication of another meaning of 长 (cháng)—length of time, —this saying implies that evildoers will soon meet their doom.

脱了裤子放屁——多费一道手续

tuōle kùzi fàngpì——duō fèi yī dào shǒuxù

Taking off the pants to break wind—make an unnecessary move

放屁不需要脱裤子。如果先把裤子脱掉,再去放屁,当然不算错,只是多费了一道手续,令人感到可笑。

这个歇后语用来比喻多此一举,自找麻烦。(含贬义)

To break wind, it is unnecessary to take off the lower garments.

This saying refers to making an unnecessary fuss over a simple matter.

外甥打灯笼——照旧(舅)

wàisheng dǎ dēnglong——zhào jiù

The nephew holds a lantern for his uncle—things stay unchanged

这是一个谐音的歇后语。"舅"和"外甥"是亲戚称呼。一个孩子，称他母亲的哥哥或弟弟为"舅"，舅舅则把他叫"外甥"。外甥打着灯笼给舅舅照明引路。由于"旧"与"舅"同音，"照舅"变成"照旧"。

"照旧"的意思是：仍旧保持从前的样子，没有一点儿变化。

This is a pun. Maternal uncle is 舅, while the son of one's sister is 外甥. Since 舅 is pronounced the same as 旧 (old, usual, unchanged), "hold a lantern for his uncle" 照舅 sounds like 照旧, which means stay unchanged, or remain as usual.

王八吃秤砣——铁了心

wángba chī chèngtuó——tiěle xīn

A tortoise swallowing a weight — get an iron heart

"王八"就是乌龟的俗称。"秤砣"是称物品时用来使秤平衡的金属锤,用铁铸成。假设一只王八把秤砣吞到肚子里,连心也变成铁的了。

"铁了心"比喻主意已定,很难改变;或比喻意志坚定,毫不动摇。

王八 is an alternative vulgar name for a tortoise. 秤砣 is the iron weight sliding along the arm of a steelyard. If a tortoise swallowed a weight, he would feel as though he had got an iron heart.

铁了心 means having made up one's mind or having an iron will.

蚊子叮菩萨——认错人了

wénzi dīng púsà——rèn cuò rén le

A mosquito bites a clay idol—mistaken identity

蚊子飞到庙里，看到一尊菩萨坐在那里，飞过去叮他的血。这才发现菩萨是泥土做的，自己错把他当成活人了。

这个歇后语用来比喻弄错了人。

A mosquito flies into a temple and tries to bite a clay idol, thinking that it is a living person.

This saying refers to the wrong identification of someone.

乌龟吃萤火虫——心里明白

wūguī chī yínghuǒchóng——xīnlǐ míngbai

A tortoise which has swallowed a firefly—bright inside

乌龟全身都是黑的,嘴里一般也不声不响。萤火虫的尾端能够发光。设想一只乌龟把萤火虫吞了下去,肚子里面也就明亮起来了。

这个歇后语用来比喻嘴里不说,心中明白,也就是"心中有数"的意思。

A tortoise is dark all over, and is always silent. If a tortoise swallowed a firefly it would be bright inside.

This saying is used to describe someone who knows something very well in his heart but remains silent about it.

瞎子戴眼镜——多此一举

xiāzi dài yǎnjìng——duō cǐ yī jǔ

A blind man putting on glasses—an unnecessary action

瞎子的眼睛看不见,戴上眼镜还是看不见。所以瞎子戴眼镜,完全是多余的举动。

这个歇后语用来比喻做多余而不必要的事情。(含贬义)

It is completely unnecessary for a blind man to wear glasses, since he cannot see anything.

This saying refers to doing something superfluous and unnecessary.

瞎子点灯——白费蜡

xiāzi diǎn dēng——bái fèi là

A blind man lighting a candle—wasting wax

蜡烛是用来照明的。瞎子眼睛看不见，用蜡烛点上灯，仍然什么也看不见，只是白白地浪费了蜡烛。

这个歇后语用来比喻白费力气，一点效果也没有。（含贬义）

Even though a blind man lights a candle in the dark he still cannot see anything; he is simply wasting the wax of the candle.

This saying indicates that someone expends his energy on something to no avail.

虾子过河——谦虚(牵须)

xiāzi guò hé——qiānxū

A shrimp crossing a river—modesty

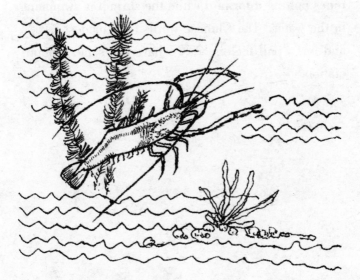

这是一个谐音的歇后语。虾子就是虾的方言。虾的头上有长短触角各一对,口语叫虾须。虾过河的时候,虾须漂浮在水面上,仿佛像两根绳子牵着虾向前游。"谦虚"与"牵须"同音,所以"牵须"变为"谦虚"。

"谦虚"的意思是虚心,不自满,肯接受别人的批评和建议。(含褒义)

This is a pun. 虾子, the dialectal name for shrimp, has feelers on its head that look like two ropes pulling it forward while the shrimp is swimming in the water. The Chinese words for "modest 谦虚" and for "pull feelers 牵须" have the same pronunciation.

瞎子磨刀——快了

xiāzi mó dāo——kuài le

A blind man sharpening a knife—not far to go (it feels sharper now)

瞎子看不见,在磨刀的时候,磨一会儿,就用手试一试刀刃,口里不住地说:"快了!快了!""快"有"锋利"和"迅速"两个意思。这里是说锋利。

这个歇后语实际表示的意思是,事情很快就要完成,或者目的地很快就要到达了。

When a blind man is sharpening a knife, once in a while he has to stop to test the blade with his finger and say repeatedly: 快了, 快了, which could mean sharp or soon. 快了 here means "soon, before long, not much left". It is used when indicating that a task will soon be done, or a goal will soon be accomplished.

鞭炮又叫爆竹,是小孩子非常喜欢的东...
放起来爆炸的声音很响,而且容易烧伤...
所以小孩子又爱它又怕它。
这个歇后语用来描述对人或对物又喜欢...
矛盾心理。

鞭炮, also called 爆竹, means firecrack...
...ren like to let off firecrackers. However, th...
...that they can be burned or otherwise injured...
...en they let them off they feel both joy and fear...
This saying is used to describe a person'...
...cting psychological state of feeling both joy and...
...t the same time.

小葱拌豆腐——一清(青)二白

xiǎocōng bàn dòufu——yī qīng èr bái

Shallot mixed with bean curd—one green and one white (completely clear-cut or innocent)

这是一个谐音歇后语。小葱是青青的，豆腐是白白的。用小葱拌豆腐，做成一道菜，有青又有白，好看又好吃。"清"与"青"同音，"一青二白"成了"一清二白"。

"一清二白"也是个成语，有两个意思：(1)清清楚楚，毫不含糊；(2)一个人很纯洁，没有污点。(含褒义)

This is a pun. Shallots are green, while bean curd is white. The dish called "shallot mixed with bean curd" is both tasty and pleasant to look at—green contrasted with white. The 青 meaning green and the 清 meaning innocent have the same pronunciation. Therefore, 一青二白 becomes 一清二白, which means "completely innocent (of the charge)" or "clear-cut, explicit, plain".

小孩儿放鞭炮——又...

xiǎoháir fàng biānpào——yòu ài yò

Kids letting off firecrackers—and fear

小和尚念经——有口无心

xiǎo héshang niàn jīng——yǒu kǒu wú xīn

An apprentice monk reciting scriptures—saying what one does not mean

小和尚初入佛门，天天跟着老和尚念经，却不懂得念的经文是什么意思，一点也不动心。

"有口无心"的意思是：(一件事情) 只是嘴上说说，并没有把它放在心里。

An apprentice monk who has just started to practice Buddhism recites scriptures with the older monks every day, but does not understand what he is saying. His heart is not moved at all.

有口无心 means speaking empty words or making insincere statements.

秀才遇见兵——有理说不清

xiùcai yùjiàn bīng——yǒu lǐ shuō bù qīng

A scholar meeting a warrior—unable to vindicate oneself against an unreasonable opponent

　　过去，人们把秀才看做是很有学问的读书人，而当兵的往往是蛮横(mánhèng)不讲理。秀才遇见兵，虽然有一肚子的道理，但总是说不清楚的。

　　这个歇后语比喻对蛮横不讲道理的人，是无法和他讲理的。

In the past a scholar was considered to be educated and cultured, while a warrior was regarded as rude and unreasonable. If a dispute arose between a scholar and a warrior, the scholar would find it hard to vindicate himself in spite of having justice on his side.

This saying implies that there is no reasoning with an unreasonable person.

哑巴吃黄连——有苦说不出

yǎba chī huánglián——yǒu kǔ shuō bù chū

A dumb person tasting bitter herbs—unable to express bitter feelings

黄连是一种非常苦的中药。哑巴吃了黄连,感到味道很苦,嘴里却说不出来。

在汉语中,"苦"有两个意思:一是味道苦(bitter),一是痛苦(pain; suffering)。这里的"有苦说不出"实际是指心中痛苦,但嘴里说不出来,或不便说出来。

Huanglian, the rhizome of Chinese gold thread, is used in traditional Chinese medicine. It tastes quite bitter. When a dumb person tastes it, he senses the bitter taste but cannot express how he feels.

苦 can mean either bitter, pain or suffering. Here in this saying, 苦 refers to the latter. It means to suffer in silence, or be unable to communicate one's suffering.

哑巴吃饺子——心里有数

yǎba chī jiǎozi——xīnlǐ yǒu shù

A mute person eating *jiaozi*—knowing how many he has eaten

哑巴吃饺子的时候,吃了多少饺子,嘴上虽然说不出来,但心里总是有个数目的。

"心里有数"的意思是:对某一种事情嘴上虽然不说,但是心里十分明白。

When a mute person eats *jiaozi* (dumplings), he knows how many he has eaten, even though he cannot speak.

心里有数 means knowing the situation quite well, yet saying nothing.

阎王爷出告示——鬼话连篇

Yánwangyé chū gàoshi——guǐhuà lián piān

The King of Hell's announcement—a whole series of lies

佛教称管地狱的神叫阎王或阎王爷。阎王爷贴出告示,告示上讲的都是鬼的事情,用的都是鬼的词语,所以说是"鬼话连篇"。

"鬼话连篇"比喻讲的全是骗人的假话、谎话。(含贬义)

In Buddhism the King of Hell is called 阎王 *Yanwang*, or 阎王爷 *Yanwangye*. An announcement by *Yanwang* should be all about ghosts' affairs and be written in ghosts' language. However, this saying is not really about ghosts, but means "a pack of lies".

张飞穿针——粗中有细

Zhāng Fēi chuān zhēn——cū zhōng yǒu xì

Zhang Fei threading a needle—subtle in one's rough ways

中国古代的三国时代，蜀国有名大将叫张飞。张飞以身材魁梧、举止粗鲁而著名。粗鲁的张飞却把细细的丝线穿入小小的针眼里，形成"粗"和"细"的有趣对比。

"粗中有细"指一个人在粗鲁之中还有精细的地方。（含褒义）

In the Three Kingdoms Period in ancient China, there was a general in the State of Shu called Zhang Fei, who was known for his stalwart appearance and rough and straightforward character. The image of him threading a needle is one of sharp contrast between subtlety and roughness.

粗中有细 means being somewhat refined in one's rough ways.

丈二金刚——摸不着头脑

zhàng èr Jīngāng————mō bù zháo tóunǎo

The giant monk's head—cannot be reached

(can't make head or tail of something)

佛教称金刚是佛主的卫士，身高为一丈二尺。身材这么高大的金刚，一般的人怎么能够摸得着他的头呢？

"摸不着头脑"的意思是：不了解情况，不清楚底细，不知道缘由等等。

金刚 was one of Buddha's warrior attendants. How could you touch his head if he were a giant? The extended meaning of 摸不着头脑 is "be in the dark, be completely at a loss".

芝麻开花——节节高

zhīma kāi huā——jiéjié gāo

Sesame in bloom—rising steadily

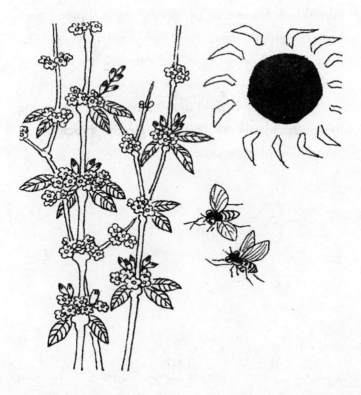

芝麻是一种一年生的草本植物，子实可以榨油。芝麻开花有一个特点：茎（jīng）往上面长一节，开一层花。茎不断地长，花不断地开。

这个歇后语用来比喻生活水平逐渐提高；也比喻人的思想、学习、技能等一天比一天进步。（含褒义）

Sesame is a plant, the seeds of which produce oil. When sesame is in bloom, each flower grows higher than the last, and the stem rises joint by joint. The flowers grow continuously as the stem rises.

This saying is used to describe either ever-rising living standards or making steady progress in thought, studies or skills.

周瑜打黄盖——一个愿打，一个愿挨

Zhōu Yú dǎ Huáng Gài——yī ge yuàn dǎ, yī ge yuàn ái

Zhou Yu beats Huang Gai — the punishment is appropriately given by one and willingly accepted by the other

中国古代的三国时代，吴国和蜀国联合抵抗曹操领导的魏国。在一次大战中，为了火攻曹操的军营，吴国大将黄盖向主帅周瑜献了"苦肉计"，让周瑜把他打得皮开肉裂，然后到曹操那里去搞假投降，以便从内部攻破曹营。

这个歇后语用来比喻在一件事情或一笔交易中双方的态度，说明双方都是心甘情愿的。

In the Three Kingdoms Period in ancient China, the State of Wu was allied with Shu against Wei, which was ruled by Cao Cao. General Huang Gai of Wu offered to have himself tortured by the commanding general Zhou Yu and then flee to Cao Cao, pretending to have gone over to the latter's side.

This saying is used to indicate that both parties are in accord on a matter of business.

猪八戒吃人参果——全不知滋味

Zhū Bājiè chī rénshēnguǒ——quán bù zhī zīwèi

Zhu Bajie eating ginseng—not knowing the taste at all

《西游记》中有一段描写猪八戒吃人参果的故事。故事说：猪八戒偷了镇元大仙种的人参果，由于贪嘴好吃，连人参果的滋味也没有尝到，就囫囵(húlún)吞下肚里。

这个歇后语用来比喻：(1) 不知道食物的滋味；(2)不知道东西的价值(不识货)。(含贬义)

Zhu Bajie is one of the chief characters in the novel *Journey to the West*. He used to be a Divine General of Heaven but was punished and reincarnated with the spirit of a pig. In the novel, there is a story about Zhu Bajie eating ginseng. Zhu Bajie, who is gluttonous, swallows up all the ginseng he stole from an immortal's orchard without knowing the taste of it.

This saying means either not appreciating the taste of food or not knowing the value of something.

囫囵：整个儿。
Whole, entirely.

猪八戒照镜子——里外不是人

Zhū Bājiè zhào jìngzi——lǐ wài bù shì rén

Zhu Bajie looking at himself in a mirror—blamed everywhere

猪八戒长着大耳朵、长嘴巴，猪头人身，面目丑恶难看。猪八戒拿着镜子照自己，镜子里面和外面都不是人的模样。

这个歇后语用来比喻里外、上下都讨不到好，夹在中间受气；或比喻处境困难，到处受到埋怨。（含贬义）

Zhu Bajie is very ugly, with a pig's head and a human body. If he looked at himself in a mirror, he could find that he was not like a human being either inside or outside the mirror.

The extended meaning of this saying is being bullied at home and outside, or being blamed everywhere.

竹篮打水——一场空

zhúlán dǎ shuǐ——yī cháng kōng

Drawing water with a bamboo basket—achieving nothing

竹篮子有许多小洞，用来打水，水都漏掉了，篮子里总是空空的。

这个歇后语用来比喻希望和努力完全落空，费了很大的劲，最后一无所获。

It is no use trying to draw water with a basket, since it has cracks, and does not allow water to remain in it.

This saying is used to describe achieving nothing in the end, though one has tried very hard.

啄木鸟找食——全凭嘴

zhuómùniǎo zhǎo shí——quán píng zuǐ

A woodpecker searching for food—all depending on the mouth

啄木鸟吃食，全靠自己坚硬的嘴，啄开树皮，捕捉树洞里的虫子。

这个歇后语用来讽刺某种人不踏踏实实地工作，只凭耍(shuǎ)嘴皮、说漂亮话过日子。

A woodpecker has to peck holes in trees with its hard beak to find insects to eat.

This saying is used to describe a type of person who merely chatters idly, and never works in a down-to-earth way. It can also mean being addicted to fine words or paying lip service.

图书在版编目（CIP）数据

歇后语 100：汉英对照 / 尹斌庸编著. - 北京：华语教学出版社, 1999.8
（博古通今学汉语丛书）
ISBN 7 - 80052 - 710 - 7

Ⅰ. 歇… Ⅱ. 尹… Ⅲ. 对外汉语教学—歇后语—对照读物—英、汉
Ⅳ. H195.5

中国版本图书馆 CIP 数据核字(1999)第 08153 号

博古通今学汉语丛书

歇后语 100

*

©华语教学出版社
华语教学出版社出版
（中国北京百万庄路 24 号　邮政编码 100037）
电话：010-68995871
传真：010-68326333
网　　址：www. sinolingua. com. cn
电子信箱：hyjx@ sinolingua. com. cn
北京外文印刷厂印刷
中国国际图书贸易总公司海外发行
（中国北京车公庄西路 35 号）
北京邮政信箱第 399 号　邮政编码 100044
新华书店国内发行
1999 年（34 开）第一版
2006 年第五次印刷
（汉英）
ISBN 7 - 80052 - 710 - 7 / H·780(外)
9 - CE - 3332P
定价：16.00 元